Munajat

Forty Prayers

Munajat

Forty Prayers

PIR ELIAS AMIDON

For information about current trainings, retreats, and
activities of the Sufi Way, visit www.sufiway.org and
www.theopenpath.org. Contact the Sufi Way by email
at info@sufiway.org, or by post at the address below.

Sufi Way Limited
2 Sente de la Pierre au Roy
60240 Tourly, France
Tel: +33 344 49 2105
www.sufiway.org

© 2017 Sufi Way Ltd.
Published by Open Path Publishing
Boulder, Colorado

Book design by Jeff Fuller

Printed in the USA

ISBN 978-1-63587-233-0

for Father Paolo Dall'Oglio

اسم الله هو السلام

God's Name is Peace

Note

The forty prayers in this little book were originally inspired by the *Munajat* — "whispered prayers," or "intimate conversations with God" — of the 12th Century Persian Sufi, Abdullah Ansari. Intimate prayer like this suits the sensibility of Sufis — Ibn Arabi, Rumi, Hafez and many others became masters of it. On the one hand praying in this manner is love-talk evoking the nearness of divine reality, and on the other hand it can't help but go mute as it points to the unspeakable majesty of the Real. It's a form of prayer that endears at the same time that it is in awe.

These prayers were written over a period of forty dawns as part of a practice (called a *chilla* in our tradition) that I gave myself. Writing them didn't feel to me like writing in the usual way — it was more like waiting. Waiting and listening. Then my heart would start whispering and I'd try to write it down. Often when a prayer came to its end I'd find it bewildering, and not very well written. I'd do my best to close my notebook then and not fuss with it. Coming back to them later I'd begin to hear what they were trying to say. My hope in sharing them with you is that they may do that for you too.

The prayers are printed here in the order they came to me over those forty dawns. The titles were added later for ease of reference.

The Secret

Beloved, I whisper to you on this pillow
and you tease me with your laugh.
My hand falls through your face.

I am not what you think, you say,
I am not a you, not inside a skin,
I am un-you, un-I, unmade.

Then why do I love you,
and what am I loving?
Beloved, who are you?

Come closer, you whisper, come here.
I will tell you, but promise me
you'll keep it a secret.

This

Closer than words that form in my mind,
closer than tongue that says them,
closer than now where everything happens,
you, my beloved, are this.

I call you gracious but that is a word,
I call you God but that's an idea,
I call you you but that is a fiction,
you, my beloved, are this.

You flare supernovas and spin every atom
and blink every eye in the world,
you lift every wing and kiss every lover,
you, my beloved, are this.

I turn to myself and ask what I am,
I ask what feels what I feel,
you don't say a word but tell me with light,
you, my beloved, are this.

Your Home

The light this morning is of this world
but I know you are here.
You are very quiet but you leave
this trace in my heart.

Between my eye and the sunlight on the floor
you are smiling, I am sure,
but who would believe me?
Oh, if I could only tell them!

You gave me this body, you gave me this me.
I want to give them back now!
My body and my self are colors of your light,
here, my beloved, they are yours!

Guide me this day with your unseen love,
guide me with your kindness,
take away my self-preoccupation,
and use my heart, beloved, for your home.

The Feathers of My Pillow

Your light fills the universe entire
yet you still find time to come to my bed,
kiss me on the forehead, and wake me.

I try to make myself up
but you undo me
like the wind takes away a sound.

I can't say anything reasonable
now that you are here.
Every time I try, you touch my lips
and make me stop.

You keep turning things inside out —
darling, look, even the feathers of my pillow
are floating away!

A little girl stamps her foot in a puddle
and laughs with delight at the splash,
just as you do in my heart.

Flag

At dawn each day I raise my heart
like a flag above my house.
Faded and thin it hangs there motionless
waiting while the first light comes.

You whisper. The flag trembles.
Your breeze arrives from nowhere.
Little waves, like old friends,
make the cloth laugh with them.

Beloved, you are so near
but I can't see you,
just this happy flapping
in the morning light.

Sama

Out of beginningless time
the bird of your love arrives
and perches here in my heart.

On its way to endlessness
it has no need for hurry.
It sings and the whole world dances!

Waves bow to their partner the shore,
stars wink and flirt with the night,
the orchard ripens, leaves spin and clap,
even the bugs turn somersaults!

I won't live forever and I don't care.
Just to hear this song, beloved,
is all the joy I could ask for.

In the Cathedral

Beloved
you strike my heart with fear
when I glimpse
the smallest corner of your immensity,
stars scattered everywhere,
galaxies flung into infinite space.

In the cathedral of your light
I am nothing.
How is it then, in your mercy,
you breathe with me here on this pillow?
How is it you care to be so intimate?
I don't understand.

Forgive my questions.
I don't need to understand.
I only need to love you
with this love that is yours.

Miserere

Before the bomb the bullet,
before the bullet the sword,
before the sword the spear,
each one made to hurt the heart
you gave each baby born.

Beloved, we are not worthy of your gifts, we are not worthy.
How you made these eyes to see, we are not worthy.
How you made these ears to hear, we are not worthy.
How you made these hands to touch, we are not worthy.

The child cries for his father shot,
huddled there in the back of the truck.
I saw him in this morning's news,
his little hand on his father's back.

Beloved, you are the one we kill,
it is your heart we break.
You are the child who cries in the truck,
you are the dust that soaks his tears.

We want to hold you, we want to rock you,
we want to take you in our arms, but
we are not, we are not, we are not worthy.
Forgive us, beloved, guide us, let us try again.

Heavy Cities

Beloved, take my sad heart into yours,
take this wounded world,
take the dark air, the heavy cities,
take the children we have blamed,
take us, take the women at their windows,
take the men who don't know what to do,
take us, beloved, into your heart,
the salmon lost, the little frog, the bees,
the coral, the whale, the falling trees,
take the streets, the asphalt, the roar of tires,
take our machines and the ones we've discarded,
take the fast missiles, take the plastic bottles,
take our plans, our broken words,
take us, beloved, into your heart,
teach us what matters.

Our Appointment

I have been waiting for you so long,
looking here and there, walking back and forth,
reading holy books, dozing off,
startled by every sound that might be your approach.

Where are you? I have tried to be faithful
to our appointment. Do I have the time right?
The place? You who knows all,
why do you leave me alone like this?

I have grown old waiting, my hair is white,
I pass the time humming songs about you
and tending the flowers I planted for you.
I thought you would like them. Where are you?

Forgive me. I know you have business
more important. I will stop complaining.
In fact, I will stop waiting too.
Just sit here like this, nothing to do.

A tear drops on the page. It isn't mine.
The page flutters. I look up. Oh!
You are the seeing. The sound of footsteps…
Oh! You are the hearing. Oh beloved!

Don't Leave Me

You open my heart as clear as the air,
you fill me with this gladness.

I thought I had to make up what happens next
but you took that job from me.

I have nothing to do! Now tell me,
who said that? You? Me? Who?

You have many lovers, but I'm not jealous,
in fact it makes me so happy
to see you walk with that old woman there,
steadying her step, kissing her hair,
waiting while she wonders where you are.

You open my heart as clear as the air,
then say, go play, go love, go care. Be like me.

Oh beloved, promise you won't leave me!
Now why are you laughing? Did I say something funny?

Darling

Darling, you know there are people in this world
who would cut out my tongue
if they heard me calling you darling.
They imagine they need to protect your honor
and I love them for that, but they needn't worry.
I mean no disrespect.

I call you darling because you're so shy,
hiding in everything the way you do,
and because of the wild nights we've had.
That kind of thing isn't easily forgotten,
is it my darling?

Come, show me again
how you turn into this pen. Ah!
And now this breath. Ah!
How do you do that?
What about this thought? This body?
Ah! That tickles!

Psalm 1

Truly you are great, beloved, and your presence infinite!

Your light reaches the darkest corners of the world,
your joy makes every atom spin.

You overturn armies with the thunder of your sorrow,
and cities awaken to the sound of your drum.

Truly you are great, beloved, and your presence unbounded!

Even the footsteps of the butterfly announce your presence,
and the trembling of its wings give proof of your love.

Oh soul of all, you lift my heart into the morning,
you close my eyes at night.

Truly you are great, beloved, your presence infinite,
and all the worlds tell of your glory!

The Dragonfly

Now that the dawn has come so gently
to the grasses at the water's edge,
my quiet soul, like the dragonfly there,
warms its wings in the morning light,
and waits to rise in your boundless air.

Lift me, beloved, show me how
to soar and dart and hover still,
or land on the grass's bowing stem,
or disappear out of sight
into your continents of light.

You are wonderful to have made me
with these transparent wings,
wonderful to have made this sky
for me to rise up through, and wonderful
to pretend that you and I are two.

The Quiet

Your stillness is upon me.

How gentle it is.
It doesn't ask anything.

It holds the beating of my heart
and the air around me.

It holds the story of my life.

So quiet, so clear,
no wonder no one notices.

Your stillness is upon me.

It comes first, gives birth,
like a mother births a child.

Mother light, child light,
the quiet at the heart.

Your stillness is upon me.

You are the I that I am.

If

If my heart was as big as yours, beloved, I would go right
now to every woman I have ever loved and every woman
I have ever wanted to love, and to every woman and
man and child I have ever met, and even to those I have
never met, the mothers and fathers, the children and
storekeepers and politicians, the people who are angry
and the people who are hurt, all of them, I would go right
now and tell them they are beloved and cherished, and
I would take their hearts into mine and pour my heart
into theirs and tell them how eternally beautiful they are,
and they wouldn't know where this message came from
but it wouldn't matter because their hearts would be
blossoming and the light from their chests and their eyes
would light up whoever came near them, and even when
the moment came for them to die they would sing out oh
beautiful! beautiful! and become happy blessing angels in
your infinite tender light, if my heart was as big as yours.

Benediction

Your dawn comes with the color of a dove
like a benediction in the air,
waking the town, swinging windows open,
freeing my heart from its shadows.

All my life, beloved, you have been patient,
pouring your light through me without my noticing.
Now all I can do is put my forehead on the floor,
like the sunlight bowing there.

I don't know where your light comes from
or where I end and you begin.
You make my heart into empty sky
and the light of your morning my home.

Wanton Love

Beloved, your love is simple
but mine has conditions.
I want things to be different,
then you go and forgive everybody!

Your sun spreads naked on every roof,
it enters every window,
sets out breakfast for the greedy and the poor,
it even warms the broken toys in the garden.

I pick and choose. You don't.
You take everyone's hand!
How could you be so wanton?
If I were like you they'd lock me up.

What's that? What did you say?
You want me to what? Well…
All right, I will. But keep it to yourself.
Don't tell.

This Doesn't Make Any Sense

Beloved, the old men said I shouldn't love you like this.
They gave me a book but I can't read that sad religion
now that you've answered our prayers.

Look! people are coming out of their houses,
kissing each other's cheeks, giving compliments,
wondering what's happening to them.

Look! the sun's turning in circles,
the ocean's waving, the birds are singing nonsense
just to see the way you smile.

I must be dreaming. This doesn't make any sense.
Shouldn't we put our clothes back on
and try to remember our names?

How It Feels

I know you are curious, beloved.
I know you want to know how it feels
to sip this tea and to hear
those raindrops tapping on my window.

I know you want to know how it feels
to stand on two feet, to walk and stop,
to turn your attention,
how it feels to laugh in good company,
and to kneel beside the dead body of a friend.

You are curious, beloved, I know,
to feel how it feels to touch with your lips
breathing skin,
to land your tenderness on just one thing.

I know you want to know
what it's like to die, to fall
into yourself with a silent shout,
and what it's like to hold a pen
and search for words in the dark.

I know you want to know.
I'd give my life to tell you.

Drunken Prayer

Today is not a day for business,
let's close the shop. No more
patient work and money worry, not today,
no more careful counting, not with you
spinning around in my heart like this.
I can't keep still. Listen!
The piano's playing all by itself!
The eggs are cooking themselves in the pan!
My holy books have jumped off their shelves,
they're flapping around the room,
pages falling everywhere. I'm happy
but don't let anyone see me like this
or the whole town will pick up its skirts and run away.
Beloved, when you kill me, I pray
I'll be just as sober as I am today.

The Nest of Nearness

An old friend of yours told me
that my heart is like a bird in the world of desire
flying in the air of seeking
until it lands in the nest of nearness to you.

I fold my wings. The nest is lined
with the soft down of silence, held
in the infinite tree of your presence.
I didn't know it would be like this.

Where I come from people are lonely.
They hurry past your beauty, fearing death.
I used to be like them, afraid of heights,
until you gave my heart these wings.

Now I don't ask to be comforted.
That would keep me scared and needy.
Now there is no edge to the peace
of my happiness and yours.

Psalm 2

My heart is your sky, beloved,
there is nothing I need.
On the hills of your earth I walk upright
and in the fields of your love I find peace.
You have made my soul
a window and opened it to you.
You have taken away my fear.
You have given me to know
my home is your presence
and I will live
in the light of your joy forever.

This Day

Gentle now, you come to me
in the quiet of the dawn.
You ask for nothing, yet I know
I must change my life.

You breathe on my complaints,
dust motes in the slant of sun,
and I can't help but smile.
The morning moves to other neighborhoods
but you linger here, waiting for me.

Beloved, I know you don't exist,
I know I have invented you
just like you've invented me,
but does it matter? We're here
waiting for each other, smiling.
Now let's see what this day brings.

Pouring

The tender one inside each one is you.
The quiet one inside each one is you.
The one I love inside each one is you.
Beloved, you pour into so many faces I forget
who I'm talking to. I want to be faithful
but you keep winking at me from all these eyes.

My heart has a confession: it's in love with the sky
and the great mountain there and the way they touch
each other here inside me. Sometimes they're so gentle
they hardly move, then soft rain runs down.
Sometimes lightning leaps up and a wild howling follows.

Beloved, you keep pouring this moment into the next
and you don't leave a clue how you do it.
I'm in love with that pouring.

Rags and Bones

I said it was me who loves you,
who calls you beloved and soul of souls,
but I'm only selling rags and bones,
shouting in the street. I don't know your glory.

I thought my shouts would endear you to me
but then you stole my cart and donkey.
Even my hat blew away. I have nothing to give you.
Love words are cheap when they're copied.

Call me an imposter, a counterfeit forger,
a vaudeville performer who forgets his lines.
I pretended to be your lover
so people would clap and you would be pleased,
but who, who made this love?
Your arrow struck me and I fell off the stage.

You, you are the lover, the beloved, the love,
you, you are this sun that burns in my heart.

Aleppo

These prayer beads I bought in Aleppo, there in
the crowded bazaar, do you remember beloved?
Bargaining with the masbaha shopkeeper, he got the
better deal, though now with the city in ruins I'm
not so sure. At least these beads escaped, repeating
God is everywhere, God is here, but their voice only
whimpers now. I tried to cheer them up, chanting
your name, but they wouldn't have it. They know
what's happened. The man's shop has been crushed,
beads scattered everywhere. Nothing moves, only
the sound of the morning's artillery thudding in the
distance. Come, beloved, let's pray together, let's pray
for the shopkeeper and his family, and the burned
awning and the broken shelves, let's pray for the beads
and the prayers they didn't say. You start. I can't find
the words.

Both Sides

Far from here you are busy with things
I don't understand. A baby being born, blood smeared,
or some old woman poking a stick in a pile of trash.
Those two lovers holding hands, did you
curl their fingers together? When they quarrel
do you take both sides? I don't understand.
This world of yours, made of all these private places,
do you expect something from us? What do you want?

Comfort only lasts so long. The baby cries,
asking for the breast to return. My life's like that,
and like the mother hurrying into the room.
Somewhere in all this commotion you're hiding a secret.
Help me find it! You keep making days and ending them
and nothing gets resolved. Is that it?
Like water going round, dripping from trees,
running to the ocean and turning into clouds?

This intricate snowflake you made into me is melting,
melting and turning into something I don't understand.
You don't care how I feel about it
since it's just you anyway, taking on shapes.
Now that's a happy thought.

At Last

Wash me, beloved, my heart is tired.
There was danger on the road,
I had to go the long way round to find you.
I'm sorry, my hair is matted and I feel old.
You'll have to scrub hard.
Pour the water of your love over my shoulders,
let it run down, let it wash through me.
You are kind to care for me so.
My burning feet are glad now, they've been so loyal,
longing to arrive at your door. They are glad now.

You are kind. You give me this robe.
You prepare a meal for me,
singing in the kitchen that song that I love.
Oh beloved, how happy I am to be here with you
in this tender light of our home at last.

Riddles

Beloved, I know you are this perfect stillness
but what's all this coming and going?
I know your presence is boundless quiet
but what's all this noise?
You cannot be seen and leave no trace
but you've filled my eyes with colors!
Not one, not two, your mystery appears and hides.
Never found, never absent, you wait for us to know
this simplest of riddles, how this, and this, are you.

We've come to think
we are alone,
outside of something holy
but could it be our privacies
are written in your heart,
and our aloneness simply holds
a mirror to your own?

Beloved, as I pray to you I hear you pray to me,
as I ask these questions you ask for me to see
you, playing in this moment, limited and free.

Tell Them

We can't remember where we came from
and the smell of spring growing in that garden.
We think this dirty city is our home.

A breeze comes in the house
and joins the stale air, forgetting the long slope of the mountain.
Now it believes in death.

Beloved, should I go out in the streets,
wave my arms, stop traffic, tell them what you told me?
They have places for people like that.

Your light is so bright it scares us
so you've put up this curtain with pretty designs.
I love watching the sun come through.

The day will come when you'll pull the curtain,
stop the traffic, and let the breeze go home.
Until that day I'll just play with these words.

No Books

Oh you who look for meaning, stop right there.
In the beloved's library there are no books.
Ink cannot tell what happens when we die.

I know you are worried, I know you don't believe
what the priests say, but don't blame them.
Watch the icicle drip, how the jewel at its tip lets go.

I went to the city of God to see what all the commotion was about,
everyone chanting and circling that famous place,
but it made me dizzy. I left lonely.

On the road home robbers took everything.
They left me for dead. When I woke up
I was on both sides of the window.

Beloved, can you say this for me?
My friend is worried. There, the hawk gliding out,
the drop falling, the word already gone, show him how that's you.

No Front or Back

Here in your heart we cast no shadow,
here we're not made of atoms and food.

Spin us around and we stay still,
hold us still and we dance.

Here where your love has no front or back,
you've made lovers able to run to each other.

Beloved, this love of yours is a riddle.
The raindrop is the ocean and the ocean the rain.

We think we need instructions but you don't help.
You just keep raining.

Trying to Make You Appear

One word at a time I dress you,
this robe, these slippers, this little earring,
all these syllables that sound like water.
I like this job but you never let me finish.
Now what am I supposed to do
with this pile of clothes on the floor?

Beloved, the sky is your raiment, brushed with gold,
and the stars beyond are sparks in your eye.
Fish gulp the air you give them —
but what do I know about it?
With a flick of their tail they're gone
and once again you escape my telling.

You don't do anything yet everything gets done.
The leaf trembles and the whole universe resounds.
I could go on like this, trying to make you appear,
but you won't have it. You smile and vanish
without stepping foot in my room, leaving only
this window open in the middle of my chest.

The Same Prayer

In the great hall of your home
our little planet sails,
a silent atom in your endlessness.

We have no idea where we are.
We pray to you but nothing answers.
Nobody knows we are here.

Your knowing and your loving
are not arranged like ours.
You're not something already made.

Beloved, you're right here breathing my body,
but you let me play on my own.
You don't know what will happen next.

This is how your love works.
It's risky, but you don't care.
We say the same prayer.

What I Want

All this talk of you as a love object
has left me on this side of the river, shouting.
Make me lose my footing, sweep me away,
fill my mouth with water and make me stop presuming.

You never fit the names we give you.
There are rumors but they don't make sense.
The Christians say Jesus and the Muslims Mohammad
since those men knew the secret of the sun's happiness.

Beloved, I know you like it when I talk to you
and even more when I stop. This pillow-talk
doesn't mean anything, that's why it's so sweet.
After lovemaking, an evening walk arm in arm.

You already know what I want most.
I want everyone to know you like this.
I'm not jealous, just the opposite.
Your love bed is big enough for everyone.

Morning sunlight pours into my room
and warms my books. They lean like drunks.
Open all the windows, let this happiness out!
We can't keep it for ourselves.

Psalm 3

Oh gracious one, your love comforts me
and your voice is tender in my heart.
The light of your morning uplifts my soul
and the color of your evening brings peace.

All my days you have accompanied me
and the kindness of your breath has given me life.
When I was lonely you reminded me,
and when I was selfish you made me see.

How often have I forgotten and lost my way,
following the signs of self-protection,
yet you have placed this shawl on my shoulders
and warmed me with your constant love.

Oh light within light, closer than now,
your wonder frees my heart,
and with every breath gives proof
there is nothing that is not you.

Your Beautiful Composure

Inside the noise my life makes
you live in silence.
You make my body move
but you stay still.
The sun climbs into the day
and everyone gets busy,
but you don't.

Over there we're hurting each other,
and over there we've left a mess,
but you don't interfere.
You're quiet, like the air,
always giving us another chance.

Teach us the way you are, beloved,
your beautiful composure, this generous giving,
the way you pour light everywhere
just to see love grow
in our gardens.

Teach us to be like that,
not asking for anything,
sweeping the kitchen after the party,
everyone home in their beds.
Teach us to turn into you
when no one's looking,
when we see stars coming out
in each other's bodies.

Dying Prayer

As you close my eyes to this world
may they open to your light,
as you stop my heart from beating
may its love for you take flight,
and lift beyond these troubles
like a song bird flying home,
to disappear in boundless joy
alone with your Alone.

Your Help

You are the becoming and the here,
the flowing and the still.
You are a you like I am an I,
empty and happy.

You don't have ears but I talk to you anyway
since we both come from the same place.
Oh beloved, I don't need you to be what I imagine,
I'm happy just to play here in your courtyard.

I want to bring you flowers
and lay them at the feet
of the people who have been kind to me
and those who haven't cared for me at all.

Look, already this morning that mountain
is up on its feet dancing around the sky.
Now the sun is getting into the act
pouring its love wine everywhere.

These dawns of yours get me drunk
and I don't know what I'm saying.
How did I end up here, so dizzy with love
I'll need your help to get me home?

Pir Elias Amidon is the spiritual director of the Sufi Way, a lineage of universal Sufism first introduced in the West in 1910 by the Indian mystic Inayat Khan. His root teacher in the order was Pir-o-Murshid Fazal Inayat-Khan. Pir Elias has also studied with Qadiri Sufis in Morocco, Theravada Buddhist teachers in Thailand, Native American teachers of the Assemblies of the Morning Star, Christian monks in Syria, Zen teachers of the White Plum Sangha, and contemporary teachers in the Dzogchen tradition. He is author of the books *The Open Path — Recognizing Nondual Awareness,* and *Free Medicine — Meditations on Nondual Awakening,* and is co-editor of the books *Earth Prayers, Life Prayers, and Prayers for a Thousand Years.* Pir Elias worked for many years in the fields of peace and environmental activism in the Middle East and Southeast Asia, and with indigenous tribes in Thailand and Burma on issues of cultural continuity and land rights. He currently leads trainings and retreats in the U.S., Britain, Holland, Germany, and Austria. For more information visit www.sufiway.org.